100 Questions and Answers About the Religiously Unaffiliated

Michigan State University
School of Journalism

Front Edge Publishing

For more information and further discussion, visit:

biasbusterguides.com

Cover design by Rick Nease
RickNeaseArt.com

Published by
Front Edge Publishing
42807 Ford Road, #234
Canton, Michigan, 48187

Front Edge Publishing books are available for discount bulk purchases for events, corporate use and small groups. Special editions, including books with corporate logos, personalized covers and customized interiors are available for purchase. For more information, contact Front Edge Publishing at info@FrontEdgePublishing.com

Contents

Acknowledgments

These are the authors of this guide. From left, top row: Chloe Peter, Salina Saleh, Jayna Bardahl and Katie Reichel. Second row: Man Liu, Alec Wycoff, Sophia Lada and Mary Kate Greene. Third row: Karly Graham, Kennedy Donoho, Evan Jones and Jakkar Aimery. Bottom row: Adrian Kresnak and Ted Wujek. Noah Hintz and Lacie Kunselman helped edit and produce this guide.

Guest speakers who joined the class on Zoom include:

Mike Lipka is an editorial manager of religion research at the Pew Research Center. The Bias Busters series often relies on Pew for its timely, nonpartisan research, including the Religious Landscape Study and other surveys.

John Hile and **Dmitri Barvinok** are principals in Front Edge Publishing. They described their unique publishing process to us and helped bring out this guide.

These allies critiqued drafts of the guide for us.

Dr. Christel J. Manning is a professor of religious studies at Sacred Heart University in Connecticut. She holds a master's degree and doctorate in religious studies from the University of California, Santa Barbara. Her latest book, "Losing Our Religion: How Unaffiliated Parents are Raising their Children," won the 2016 Distinguished Book Award from the Society for the Scientific Study of Religion.

Dr. Ariela Keysar is an associate research professor of public policy and law and associate director of the Institute for the Study of Secularism in Society and Culture at Trinity College in Hartford, Connecticut. She was a principal investigator of the American Religious Identification Survey 2008, the largest survey of religion in the United States. Keysar is co-editor of "Secularism, Women & The State: The Mediterranean World in the 21st Century," "Secularism and Science in the 21st Century" and "Secularism & Secularity: Contemporary International Perspectives."

Dr. Ani Sarkissian is an associate professor of political science at Michigan State University. She specializes in the study of religion and politics, democratization, authoritarianism and civil society. She is the author of "The Varieties of Religious Repression: Why Governments Restrict Religion."

Hemant Mehta is editor and co-host of the friendlyatheist.com and appears on the Atheist Voice channel on YouTube. Mehta has served on the board of the Foundation Beyond Belief and the Secular Student Alliance. He is the author of "I Sold My Soul on eBay" and "The Young Atheist's Survival Guide."

Mandisa Thomas, a native of New York City, is a founder and president of Black Nonbelievers, Inc. (blacknonbelievers.org). Thomas has been on CBS Sunday Morning, CNN.com, Playboy, The Humanist and in JET magazine. She is on the boards of the American Humanist Association and American Atheists. Thomas was the Unitarian Universalist Humanist Association's 2018 Person of the Year. In 2019, she was the Freedom From Religion Foundation's Freethought Heroine and the Secular Student Alliance's Backbone Award winner.

Martin Davis is a journalist who has reported on education, sports and society, and religion and society for more than 20 years. His work has appeared in the National Journal, U.S. News & World Report, National Review, Philanthropy, PGA Tour Magazine and Read the Spirit. He coaches special teams at Riverbend High School in Virginia and is the author of "Thirty Days with America's High School Coaches," published by Front Edge Publishing.

One published source among the many that helped us with answers deserves mention. It is "Reality Check," the American Atheists' 2019 U.S. Secular Survey. It polled nearly 34,000 atheists, agnostics, humanists, freethinkers, skeptics and others.

Finally, we wish to thank MSU School of Journalism professor and director **Dr. Tim P. Vos** for his support of the Bias Busters series.

Foreword

By Dr. Phil Zuckerman

Some 15 years ago, while living in Denmark, I was on a train going from Copenhagen to Aarhus. It's about a three-and-a-half-hour ride. In my compartment, sitting next to and across from me, were three Swedish women in their 30s. They were heading to a conference for physical therapists. We got to chatting.

They explained they enjoyed working with people who had various physical challenges; they found it satisfying to help others improve their quality of life. They also told me about their respective families — boyfriends, spouses, children. As they asked me about myself, I explained I was a sociologist living in Denmark for the year, doing research on Scandinavian culture and society. When they asked me to explain further, I said I was studying religion and secularity, specifically. This was met with silent stares. It was as if I had just said I was studying the latest innovations in cardboard manufacturing or the temperature fluctuations of protoplasm. They simply had nothing to say on the topic.

"Are you religious?" I asked them.

"No," was the simple response.

"I see. But do you believe in God?" I asked.

Two of the women immediately said, "No."

But the third hesitated.

"I've actually never been asked that question before," she said. "I've never thought about it. Let me think about it."

So, we all sat there in silence, while she looked out the train window, considering the prospect of the existence of God.

After about a minute or so of pondering, she said, "No, I don't."

And then we proceeded to talk about other things.

The main point of this recollection: here were three women living normal lives, finding satisfaction in their careers, helping others heal, raising children, occasionally traveling, loving partners and spouses, appreciating friends, etc. — and all without any religion. Indeed, one of the women lived such a religion-less existence that well into her 30s, she had never seriously even pondered whether or not she believed in God! Prayer, heaven, hell, Satan, the Bible, angels, demons, sin, miracles, church — none of these phenomena had any real meaning — or even place — in the lives of these Swedes. And while these women may seem totally unfathomable to many Americans, the demographic reality is that in many parts of the world, such secular identities are extremely common. For example, in many countries, such as Sweden, Denmark, Norway, Scotland, Estonia, Japan, the Netherlands, the Czech Republic, Taiwan, Vietnam and South Korea, being nonreligious is actually the dominant orientation. More people live their lives without religion than with it. We're talking hundreds of millions of people. And in many more countries, such as Uruguay, Canada, Spain, New Zealand, Chile, Hungary and Ukraine, secular people comprise a very sizable minority.

Here in the United States, there are currently around 85 million people who are nonreligious. Not all of them are atheists or agnostics — but a significant chunk is. And, like elsewhere around the world, their numbers have been growing steadily for at least 50 years. Indeed, when I was born back in the 1960s, only about 1 in 20 Americans were nonreligious, but today, the ratio is nearly 1 in 3.

Given that so many people in the world live their lives without religion, and given that their numbers are growing in just about every nation on Earth, it is crucial that we understand them. Who are they? How do they live their lives? What do they believe?

Understanding secular people is important for many reasons. For one thing, secular movements, leaders, values and ideals play significant roles in the political landscapes of the world. From the first sentence of the First Amendment to the U.S. Constitution, to Article 20 of Japan's Constitution, from France's laïcité to Vietnam's atheistic dictatorship, and from the founding of the Mexican Republic to India's current political struggles, secularism is a central pillar of both stability as well as conflict in many countries.

Additionally, secular men and women are often unjustly stigmatized as immoral scoundrels or angry curmudgeons — negative stereotypes that don't actually accord with reality yet prove to be both persistent and pernicious. For instance, in some societies, such as Saudi Arabia, Pakistan and Malaysia, hatred and fear of the secular are so strong that those who don't believe in God can be imprisoned, tortured or even executed. Here in the United States, many state constitutions – such as those of Tennessee, Texas and Mississippi, currently outlaw anyone who doesn't believe in God from holding any publicly elected office.

The goal of any social science is to understand humans: what they do, what they think and what they believe. As more and more people live their lives without religion, it is important to understand secularity. This book is a wonderful, accessible, informative addition to that endeavor.

Dr. Phil Zuckerman is professor of sociology and secular studies at Pitzer College, Claremont, California. He is also a regular affiliated professor at Claremont Graduate University and has been a guest professor for two years at the University of Aarhus, Denmark. He is the author of several books, some of which are in this guide's bibliography. They include "The Nonreligious: Understanding Secular People and Societies" and "What it means to be Moral: Why Religion is Not Necessary for Living an Ethical Life." Zuckerman also spoke to the Bias Busters class for this guide.

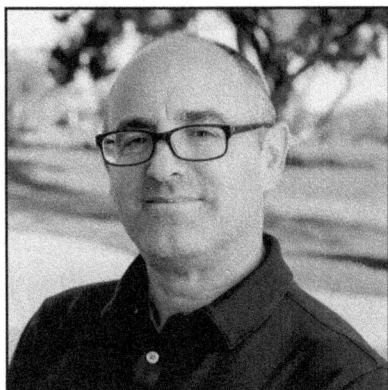

Introduction

By Dr. Morgan Shipley

Each semester, I include a common assignment in my religious studies courses. I challenge students to write a self-addressed letter that considers what they understand terms such as religion, faith, belief and spirituality to mean. Ranging from devotionals to declarations of nonbelief, these often-personal narratives reveal much about our contemporary moment and even more about the complexity of identifying with and/or denying religious affiliation. These letters go beyond simple reflections. They illustrate how many struggle to connect with systems of belief many assume to be simply natural. The letters also outline the challenges and frustrations many feel when encountering moral codes or rituals that fail to address their specific circumstances, needs or understandings of right and wrong.

From rituals such as prayer or meditation, to belief structures that outline the truth of the divine or the conditions of the afterlife, being religious brings forth an array of associated ideas and practices that require ongoing negotiations. Individuals find themselves caught between the expectations of a system they were often born into and the effects of a constantly changing world. This is complicated further within social systems that normalize religious life without necessarily defining what exactly "being religious" means. From shifts in technology to changing understandings of humans' place within the natural world, the certainty of belief fluctuates. For many, religion offers necessary grounding, solid footing to navigate the world. For others, however, the effects of these fluctuations challenge the reasonableness of belief and the value of religious practice.

The United States speaks to this dynamic. What was once considered to be a cultural given, religion as a defining mark of citizenship, remains hardly consistent throughout American history. While the majority of original colonies were founded by groups seeking freedom of religious practice, the United States Constitution promises both the free exercise of personal religion as well as the rejection of any established national religious identity. This, of course, hardly prevents many from understanding America as a "Christian nation."

At the same time that the U.S. government was imprinting God on currency in the 1950s, the effects of secularization and the move away from religion became more acute. Beginning in the 1960s, an increasing number of surveys and studies outline a growing segment of the American populace who identify as "religiously unaffiliated," "atheist" or "nonreligious." While often associated with nonbelief, these categories indicate Americans who express varying feelings about religion, from those who discard belief altogether to others who do not claim religious affiliation. It doesn't necessarily mean one lacks faith, belief or an expression of spirituality.

For the more than 85 million Americans who identify as nonreligious, we witness a turn to secularization as both an explanation for the lack of belief and a source for fulfilling the areas of life commonly associated with religion, such as morality, togetherness and agency. For the nonreligious, then, we find more than a rejection of God and faith. Instead, we uncover various ways humans highlight virtue, pursue a sense of belongingness, celebrate progress and rely on rational discourse to construct meaningful and morally driven lives.

Distinctly, secularity does not necessarily preclude religiosity, but broadly speaking, it operates by situating one's belief or sense of spirituality privately. Being religious impacts one's individual values but cannot and should not be the driving force and determining factor within the public sphere. No simple binary exists between the religious and nonreligious, between belief and nonbelief. Rather, there is an ever-adapting spectrum of orientations as contemporary people seek to understand themselves, their relationship to others, and their place within local, national, global and even universal spaces.

"100 Questions and Answers About the Religiously Unaffiliated" captures this dynamism through the voices of those who find themselves bound to a world that continues to divide and organize people according to belief and nonbelief. Through this engagement, what we discover is not simply a description of atheism and agnosticism as it relates to secularization, but the way in which individuals negotiate, adapt and respond to living both with and beyond religion.

Dr. Morgan Shipley is the Inaugural Foglio Endowed Chair of Spirituality and associate chair of religious studies at Michigan State University. Shipley's research explores secular spirituality, new religious movements and individuals who increasingly identify as spiritual but not religious.

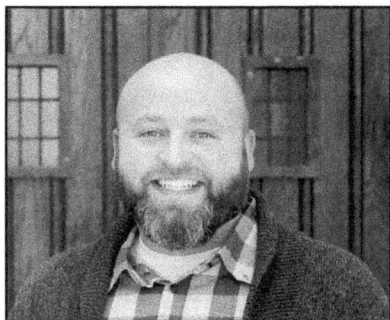

Preface

By Joe Grimm

Late in 2021, 29 percent of U.S. adults described themselves as religiously unaffiliated, according to the Pew Research Center. This shift to secularism continues. In 2019, trend lines in the U.S. General Social Survey converged. The rising number of religiously unaffiliated people had by then met declining numbers of Catholics and of evangelical Christians. When Pew first started looking at the trend in 2007, 16 percent of U.S. adults had put themselves in this broad category.[1][2]

Many of the new nonreligious had come from those Catholic and evangelical churches.

While the U.S. Constitution does not mention God or a divinity, every state constitution does. We created this guide to help replace suspicion and stereotype with understanding.

This group, like any group of some 85 million people, is intricate. Many paths lead to religious nonaffiliation, and there are many identities under that umbrella.

We will explore who is included among the nonreligious. We will learn about what they value. We will see how they deal with being outsiders in a country where religious freedom is valued but freedom from religion can be discouraged.

Chances are you know some, even if you aren't aware of it. More than 40 percent of respondents in the American

---

1 news.gallup.com/poll/467354/childhood-churchgoing-habits-fade-adulthood.aspx
2 news.gallup.com/opinion/polling-matters/406544/slowdown-rise-religious-nones.aspx

Atheists' U.S. Secular Survey of 34,000 unaffiliated people said they conceal their religious identities at work or school.

Madalyn Murray O'Hair, whose lawsuit ended mandatory prayer in public schools in 1963, was called "the most hated woman in America" in Life magazine.

For much of 2020, the Secular Coalition for America's website directory listed its communications consultant as "Anonymous," but no name. According to the site, "unwarranted prejudices and discriminatory practices ... affect atheists and humanists. Consequently, s/he felt it was best to be incognito for now, since working for an organization that protects the rights of nontheists might result in lost opportunities with other clients."

Some people we interviewed said they had been "in the closet" about their nonreligious status. Several said the road to nonaffiliation was long and rough. Many chafe under everyday slights and stereotypes.

In Alabama, voter registration forms ask people to take an oath in which they swear "so help me God." It is not enforceable, but there it is, still on the books.

Maryland's Constitution bars nonbelieving jurors and witnesses. In the U.S. Congress, where other kinds of diversity have flowered, only one member openly says she does not affiliate with any organized religion. Several others just won't say. And it's no wonder. Almost half of U.S. voters in a 2019 poll said they would vote for people of any race or religion — but not an atheist.

One former Christian we interviewed said people who question his position cannot accept that his decision has nothing to do with their beliefs. He longs for people who will hear him out and just let him talk about what IS there for him rather than what they think he lacks. And that is what we are trying to do. We want to listen. This guide is for people who want to understand.

The method in this Michigan State School of Journalism series is to interview people about what they would like others to know about them. We distill those interviews into 100 basic questions. Then we look for answers. We hope our Bias Busters guides encourage people to have more meaningful conversations with friends and acquaintances. We hope to ease reluctance that comes from not wanting to hurt others or embarrass ourselves. We think you'll find, as we have, that although we are different, we are more alike than not.

"100 Questions and Answers About the Religiously Unaffiliated" can be a first step. We hope it leads to a good conversation with one person, and then another and another. We have learned that once you know what one person thinks, all you know is what one person thinks.

Joe Grimm
Series founder and editor
School of Journalism
Michigan State University

Identities

1 Who is under the umbrella of the nonreligious?

Nonreligious Americans include atheists, agnostics, humanists, free-thinkers, skeptics, secularists and people who claim no affiliation. In the 2019 American Atheists' U.S. Secular Survey of 34,000 nonreligious Americans, atheists were the dominant group. It showed 57.1 percent of respondents identified strongly as atheists and 94.8 percent identified as atheist to at least some extent. Other identities people cited were:

Humanists   14.2%
Nonreligious 7.1%
Agnostics   6.9%
Skeptics   5.4%
Freethinkers 5.2%
Secular   4.0%

Dr. Ariela Keysar notes that the American Religious Identification Survey of 2008 indicates differences between what people say they believe and how they identify. Additionally, there are differences within categories. Some agnostics say there is no such thing as God and others say they are not sure. Another professor said there is as much diversity among the nonreligious as there is among the affiliated.

2 What is an atheist?

An atheist does not actively believe in gods. Atheism is not necessarily disbelief or denial, nor is it a religion. It rejects the assertion that gods must exist. Atheism can describe humanists and free-thinkers, as well.

3 Who are agnostics?

Agnosticism comes from a Greek word that means "unknown or unknowable." An agnostic does not have a stance on whether God or a higher power exists. Agnostics base their thinking on evidence and what they know as facts. It is not that they do not believe in gods. Instead, they just don't see evidence that supports or refutes the existence of gods.

4 In what other ways do they differ?

Atheism deals with what one believes. Agnosticism deals with what is known. Atheism is rooted in a lack of belief. Without evidence, agnostics neither believe nor disbelieve in a god or a higher power. They seek evidence. Agnosticism is not a milder or halfway form of atheism. These are different ideas altogether. People reach these conclusions from different paths. Atheists believe there is no God or gods. Agnostics are unsure because they do not see the evidence or reason to either believe or disbelieve in God's existence.

5 Who are humanists?

Humanists International is an association of 130 organizations. It declares humanism "stands for the building of a more humane society through an ethic based on human and other natural values in the spirit of reason and free inquiry through human capabilities. It is not theistic, and it does not accept supernatural views of reality." Harvard University's Pluralism Project says humanists prioritize "reason, scientific critique, civil freedoms, compassion and pragmatic ethics."

6 Who are secularists?

Secularism has several meanings. Secularism is about government and religion, but it applies to things besides people and politics. A song or piece of literature can be secular, meaning its content is not religious. Political secularism is the separation of religion from government, as Thomas Jefferson advocated. Secular studies professor and author Phil Zuckerman says secularists believe there should be no place for religion in a country's social and political affairs. Secularists want all people to enjoy freedom of thought and be allowed to choose their own beliefs. Politically, they support the separation of church and state in both government and public spheres. Skeptical secularists want to debunk religion and see its power diminished. Philosophical or ideological secularism seeks to reduce the credibility and influence of religion in society. And cultural or demographic secularism is the process by which the influence of religion in a society decreases. This is called secularization. Secularism is not atheism. Secular humanists have a wider range of beliefs than atheists but believe there is no supreme being or afterlife.

7 Who are freethinkers?

Definitions can overlap. Freedom From Religion Co-President Dan Barker writes that freethinkers "form opinions about religion on the basis of reason, independently of tradition, authority or established belief." According to Barker, freethinkers include atheists, agnostics and rationalists, provided they do not enforce conformity to any scripture or god.

8 What is irreligion?

Irreligion is not a faith identity. It is an attitude toward religion that stems from indifference or hostility. Some people have used the term to mean nonreligious. In conversation, it is a good idea to ask people to define their terms.

9 Who are "the nones?"

This term has been used to reference individuals who do not identify with any religion. It's a broad term used to describe all nonreligious individuals. Researchers understand the term as people who would respond "none of the above" when asked what religion they belong to. It is a catchy title for studies and books. When people first hear it, it can be confused with "nuns." Some nonreligious people say the label is offensive and diminishes them, implying that if they do not ascribe to an organized religion, they are nothing or zero. The nonreligious do have beliefs, just not in conventional religions.

Religious identification of the nones

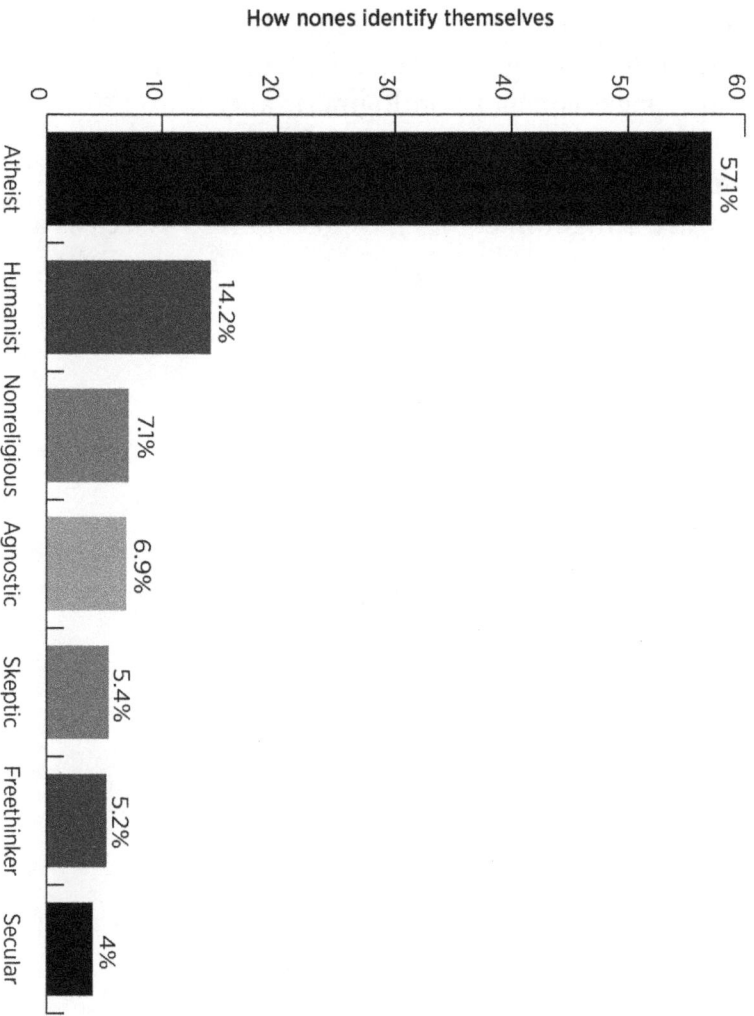

How nones identify themselves

Category	Percentage
Atheist	57.1%
Humanist	14.2%
Nonreligious	7.1%
Agnostic	6.9%
Skeptic	5.4%
Freethinker	5.2%
Secular	4%

Source: 2019 U.S. Secular Survey

Graphic by Karly Graham

10 Are Pagans and Wiccans nonreligious?

Although they do not believe in God, these groups are considered to be religions. Pagan Federation International describes paganism as a nondogmatic ancestral polytheistic or pantheistic religion that finds divinity in nature. Wicca is under this umbrella. United States and United Kingdom courts have recognized Wicca as a religion.

Beliefs

11 What does it mean to be spiritual but not religious?

Some people have profound spiritual feelings and beliefs that do not come from organized religion. Many nonreligious people believe in God and see religion as interfering with that relationship. Others find spirituality in the natural world or the human community. It is a mistake to assume one must belong to a particular religion, created by humans, to have a spiritual life. Many believe in God and pray. Their issue is with religion, not God.

12 Do nonreligious people believe life has meaning?

Certainly. Many people find deep meaning in their daily lives, families, relationships and work. While some people believe that life on Earth is lived to earn something later, others believe rewards happen as one lives. There can be great meaning and rewards in the moment. Some nonreligious people, seeking proof, rely on what is known rather than what is believed. Freethinkers say meaning begins in the mind and that people find purpose within their own minds because the universe is mindless.

13 Do the nonreligious anticipate an afterlife?

Many do, according to the 2014 Pew Religious Landscape study of more than 35,000 people. Among people who said they did not belong to an organized religion, 37 percent said they believed in heaven. About one quarter said they believed in hell. Pew found that 82 percent of religiously affiliated Americans believed in heaven, a number that had held steady since 2007.

14 What do nonreligious people think happens to us when we die?

That depends. Of the two-thirds who do not believe in an afterlife, some say they just do not know what happens or whether anything happens after life on Earth. Others say they do not see any evidence of an afterlife. They believe we simply cease to exist or rejoin the natural world in the way other living things do.

15 Do nonreligious people think there is a higher power?

In that Pew survey, people who were not affiliated with an organized religion were less likely to believe in God than those with affiliations. Even so, most religiously unaffiliated people said they, too, believed in God. The difference is that the unaffiliated are far less religiously observant.

16 Why do people oppose religions?

According to Pew research, many people give more than one reason. These are the top reasons they give:

They question the teachings	60%
They don't like church positions on social and political issues	49%
They don't like the religion	41%
They don't believe in God	37%
They feel religion is irrelevant	36%
They don't like the religious leaders	31%

People also leave religion in different ways. Some have an abrupt break after a bad event. Others leave after a long search that may have begun early in their lives.

17 Are children in certain religions more likely to leave their parents' faith?

According to a 2019 study, teens usually follow their parents' choice on religions. Pew reported highly religious parents are less likely than nonreligious parents to have teens who share their beliefs. There are differences among Protestants. About 80 percent of parents who identify as evangelical Protestant have a teen who identifies that way as well. In mainline Protestant families, 55 percent of parents have teens who identify with their beliefs. Twenty-four percent have unaffiliated teens. A 2019 Public Religion Research Institute study found about 62 percent of U.S. people who leave a faith group and become nonreligious do so before they turn 18. Another 28 percent said they did it between the ages of 18 and 29.

18 How do nonreligious people believe the universe was created?

They have different theories on creation, just as there are various theories among people who believe the universe was created by God. One answer is that no one really knows. This might come up in answer to questions like, "If it wasn't God, then who?" Some cite the Big Bang theory and Darwinism as partial explanations but say the whole story is unknown.

Nones upbringing

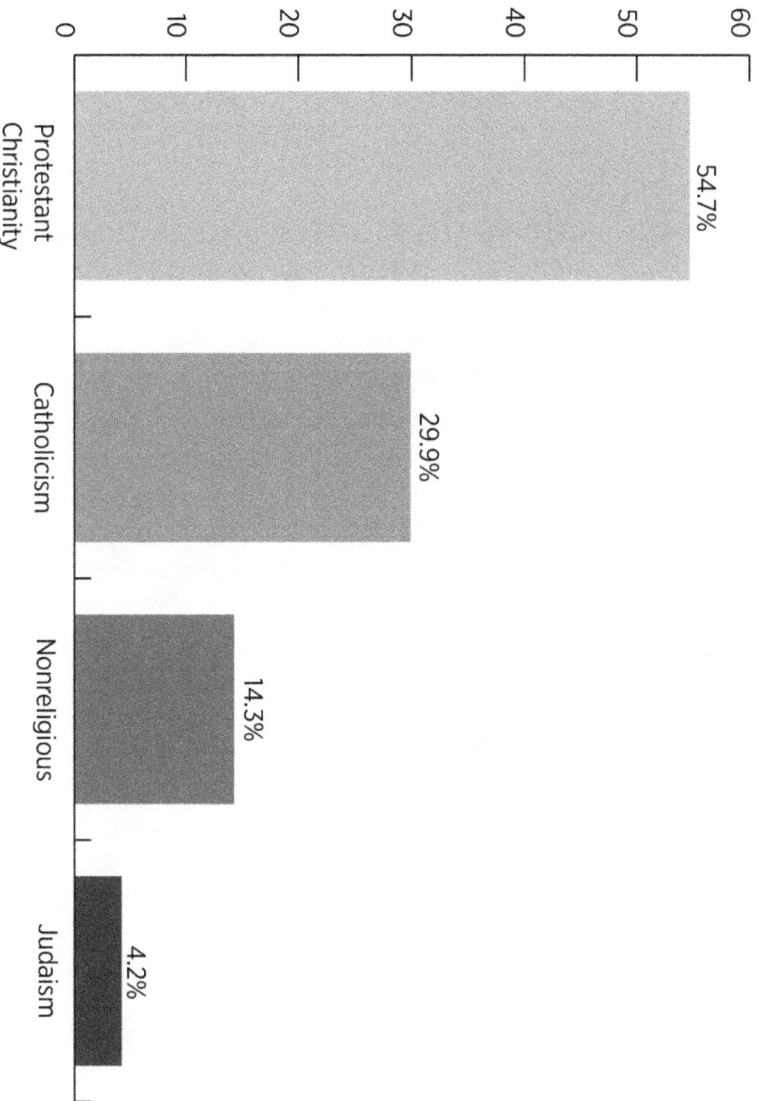

Protestant Christianity — 54.7%
Catholicism — 29.9%
Nonreligious — 14.3%
Judaism — 4.2%

Source: 2019 U.S. Secular Survey

Graphic by Karly Graham

Values

19 What values do nonreligious people hold?

Some nonreligious people say using a religion's prescription can get in the way of developing one's own moral code and values. Professor Phil Zuckerman says nonreligious people live by values like anyone else. In his book, "What it Means to be Moral: Why Religion is Not Necessary for Living an Ethical Life," he lists "The Secular Seven" values. They are:

- freethinking
- living in reality
- here-and-nowness
- empathy
- acceptance of existential mystery
- scientific empiricism
- cosmopolitanism

20 How can people without religion have morality?

Some nonreligious people say humans can make their own morality. Many use "secular" morality. This posits that if humans cooperate in a society, then they typically get along. This maximizes happiness and minimizes sadness. Some people turn this question around and ask, "How can you have morality WITH religion?" They ask whether people can have personal morals if they get theirs from a list.

21 Can the world have justice without religion or God?

Those are two very different issues. Grave injustices have long been and are still committed in the name of religion. Sometimes, religion is hijacked for unjust political purposes. Many people who have left religions say they did so because they thought the group acted unjustly. As for God's role in justice, some nonreligious people say that justice is rooted within ourselves and our social, communal and civil structures.

22 Where do nonreligious people look for hope?

Many nonreligious people consider their issues to be their own to solve. They realize they are going through something that will eventually pass. A global Pew study found that religiously affiliated people were about 25 percent more likely than the unaffiliated to say they were very happy. There was not a correlation between religion and good feelings about health.

23 How do nonreligious people cope in a crisis?

Hoping and coping are similar. Instead of looking to a higher power to fix their issues, the nonreligious are more likely to rely on themselves to deal with problems.

24 Where do nonreligious people find community?

This is of special interest in the United States, which relies more than many other countries for religious communities to connect people. That is because the country is large, people are mobile, and the population is comparatively more diverse. This increases the need for community structures. However, there are institutions beyond churches, temples and mosques that can provide them. The American Atheists Reality Check study found that more than 20 percent of respondents were involved with a local secular organization. There was also wide interest in advocacy, community, educational and service organizations. Almost three-fourths of participants were interested in more nonreligious resources for their children. Some parents said secular organizations are supportive and help reduce loneliness and depression.

Reasonings behind being unaffiliated

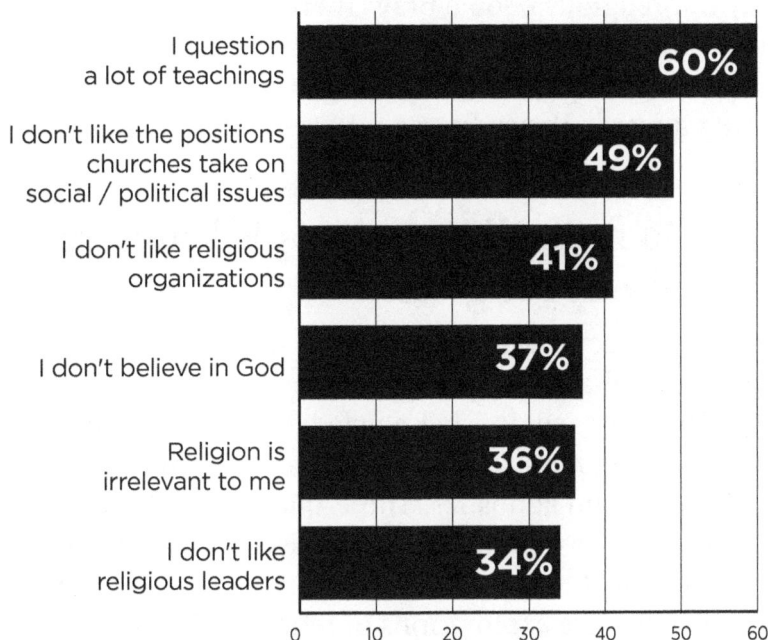

Reason	Percentage
I question a lot of teachings	60%
I don't like the positions churches take on social / political issues	49%
I don't like religious organizations	41%
I don't believe in God	37%
Religion is irrelevant to me	36%
I don't like religious leaders	34%

Source: Pew Research Center and World Religion Database

25 How does one respectfully console a nonreligious person?

Telling a nonreligious person that you will pray for them can seem insensitive and condescending. It is more sensitive to be there for them, to listen and to ask whether you can help. Many sympathy cards are nonreligious or let you write your own message.

26 Do nonreligious people pray?

Many nonreligious people pray. There is a spectrum of nonreligious practices. Those who are more spiritual may pray to a higher power. Others might experience this as looking inward. They may see this as talking to themselves.

27 Do nonreligious people know very much about religion?

Unaffiliated people knew more about religions than most religiously affiliated people, according to a 2019 Pew study. The most religiously knowledgeable of all groups, which included many Christian denominations, were Jews, atheists and agnostics. Three-quarters of those who identified as unaffiliated were raised Christian and are knowledgeable about those faiths. Some others went through extensive explorations of religions before deciding to be nonreligious.

28 Are nonreligious people charitable?

This concern is growing, along with the nonreligious share of the U.S. population. The Philanthropy Roundtable reports that "religion motivates giving more than any other factor." In 2017, a report by the Giving USA Foundation and the Lilly Family School of Philanthropy put numbers to this. The study found that the average annual contribution of nonreligious households was $695, compared to $1,590 for religious households, regardless of affiliation or identity. Religiously affiliated individuals are more than two times more generous with their financial contributions on average than those without a religious affiliation. Another concern is that some of the largest charities in the United States are faith-based. While secular people do support religious organizations whose work they admire, religious people also give to secular causes. There is crossover in both directions.

Demographics

29 What explains the rapid growth of this group?

People born after 1980 are more likely than older age groups to identify as nonreligious. Two-thirds of Millennials raised unaffiliated are still unaffiliated. This is a higher retention rate than for most major religious groups — and much higher than for older generations of nonreligious people. In 2022, Gallup senior scientist Frank Newport offered another explanation. He noted that Gallup's percentages of religiously unaffiliated people had stabilized around 20 percent between 2017 and 2022. He hypothesized that the numbers reflect rising cultural acceptance of being nonreligious. This increased people's comfort levels in telling this to researchers. He foresees growth in nonaffiliation.

30 Is there a generation gap in U.S. religious membership?

There appears to be. About 35 percent of people aged 18-29 identified as religiously unaffiliated in a Pew survey. The figure for people aged 30-49 was similar at 37 percent. These rates are almost double the 19 percent for people between the ages of 50 and 64 and four times the 9 percent of people ages 65 and up. The change accelerates as the population ages. At the end of 2021, new Pew research showed that 29 percent of all adults identified as atheists, agnostics or "nothing in particular."

31 If the unaffiliated are growing, which groups are shrinking?

Late in 2021, Pew noted declines among Protestants. This included Baptists, Methodists, Lutherans, Presbyterians and other denominational and nondenominational people. In 10 years, the U.S. percentage identifying as Protestant fell from 50 percent to 40 percent. The Catholic proportion, which had shrunk from 2007 to 2014, then stabilized. It was at 21 percent from 2014 through 2021.

32 Do nonreligious people come from religious homes?

About 55 percent of respondents to the 2019 U.S. Secular Survey said they were raised in Protestant households. About 30 percent were raised in Catholic households. One in seven participants in the survey came from nonreligious households. More than a third of respondents' religious expectations relaxed as they were growing up. About 27 percent said household expectations were firm, and about 14 percent said they were very strict.

33 What are the sizes of groups that make up the unaffiliated?

Sizes for unaffiliated groups are difficult to determine because so many people identify with more than one. In the 2019 U.S. Secular Survey, more than three quarters of participants identified as nonreligious, atheist and secular. About 60 percent of respondents said their primary nonreligious identity was atheist, and about 95 percent said they were atheist to some extent. Participants did not identify as agnostics (35 percent) to the extent that they did with other identities such as freethinker, humanist or skeptic, each with 60-65 percent.

34 What is the racial or ethnic makeup of this group?

More than two thirds of religiously unaffiliated Americans are White. Thirteen percent are Latino, according to the Pew Research Center. The percentage of unaffiliated people who are Black, Asian or of other races is less than 10 percent. However, the unaffiliated are becoming more ethnically and racially diverse. In 2007, the group was 73 percent White; in 2014, it was 68 percent White.

35 What is the group's makeup by gender?

According to Pew, 57 percent of nonreligious Americans are men, and 43 percent are women. This figure remained stable from 2007 to 2014.

Percent of religiously unaffiliated individuals by generation

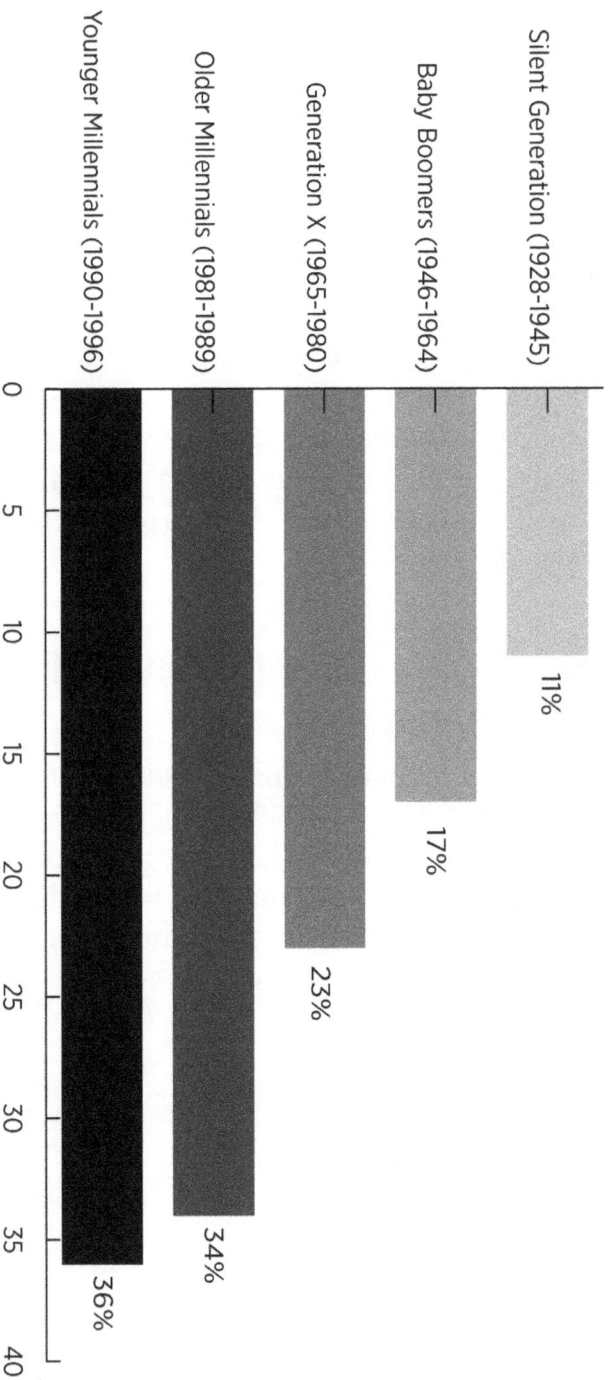

Silent Generation (1928-1945) — 11%

Baby Boomers (1946-1964) — 17%

Generation X (1965-1980) — 23%

Older Millennials (1981-1989) — 34%

Younger Millennials (1990-1996) — 36%

0   5   10   15   20   25   30   35   40

Source: Pew Research Center and World Religion Database

Graphic by Karly Graham

36 Are certain areas of the United States more religious than others?

According to Pew, Vermont and New Hampshire have the highest percentages of religiously unaffiliated Americans at 37 percent and 36 percent, respectively. Thirty percent or more of people in the Northeast states of Massachusetts, Maine, Vermont and New Hampshire identify as nonreligious. This is also true in the Northwest states of Oregon, Washington and Montana. Alabama is the most religious state with just 12 percent identifying as nonreligious. Twenty-one states spread throughout the country have 20 percent or fewer of their populations identifying as nonreligious.

37 Are religiousness and level of education related?

About 59 percent of religiously unaffiliated Americans surveyed over age 24 have a bachelor's degree or higher education. Fewer than 8 percent had a high school degree or less. This means the nonreligious generally had more education than the national average and more than the level for most religions. However, correlation does not always mean one factor causes the other.

Policy Issues

38 What are policy priorities for this group overall?

The Secular Survey found the top policy priorities of nonreligious Americans was the elimination of religious exemptions that allow for discrimination. Access to abortion and contraception are also policy priorities. More than half of people surveyed said that maintaining secular public schools should be a priority. Secularists support environmental policies that address such issues as global warming. They also promote sex education, access to abortion and protecting youth from religious harm.

39 Why is the environment high on this agenda?

Members of these groups are evidence-centric. Others find spirituality in the natural world rather than in a supreme being. Both philosophies put a high premium on science and climate issues.

40 What are key issues for atheists?

To better represent all citizens, atheists want the government to be free of religious influence. They oppose laws that include exceptions based on religion. Atheists say religious beliefs should not be the basis for government policies.

41 How do nonreligious people feel about same-sex marriage?

Nonreligious people generally see religion-based restrictions on individual rights as violations of civil rights. This means they generally support the legalization of same-sex marriage.

42 Where are nonreligious people on abortion?

This is another area where civil rights are cited. There are different opinions on how appropriate an abortion is depending on the state of a fetus. Many nonreligious people believe abortion should be an individual choice.

Church and State

43 What is "the establishment clause?"

This is the first part of the First Amendment to the U.S. Constitution. It says, "Congress shall make no law respecting an establishment of religion, or prohibiting the free exercise thereof ..." Written primarily by James Madison, it enshrined the idea that the new nation should have no nationally established church. The amendment applies only to the federal government, but the ideal has been carried to states. Courts have consistently concluded that the clause bars the government from requiring attendance or support of a religious institution. The government may not exclude some religious entities from benefits without solid secular justification. Cases come up frequently. One of the hottest was a 1962 Supreme Court ruling against mandatory school prayer. In 2022, the court supported a Washington state public high school football coach who held prayers at midfield after games.

44 Does the First Amendment protect nonreligiousness?

Secular groups argue that freedom of religion and freedom from religion must go hand in hand. They have gone to court to ensure this is so. They are concerned the federal government applies the establishment clause selectively to let religion intrude on the public sphere. Some say the clause is used to favor some religions over others or over nonreligion. Secularists would like a uniform, across-the-board separation of church and state.

45 How does the government support religion?

For the unaffiliated, these are major concerns:

- financial aid to religious education or to religious institutions
- government-sponsored prayer
- government ownership or sponsorship of religious symbols

46 Why do people oppose these?

Besides violating and weakening the establishment clause, government favoritism can legitimize religions and delegitimize individual freedoms. This is seen as a violation of First Amendment rights to be free of government rulemaking. It can also require nonreligious people to support religions, because they are tax exempt.

47 What is the problem with religious displays on public property?

Religious displays such as crosses that are publicly funded or maintained on government buildings or land imply favoritism and endorsement. Secular or nonreligious displays, even for religious holidays, have been allowed.

48 Is there a "war on Christmas?"

During his 2016 campaign, Donald Trump said there was a "war on Christmas." He vowed to restore the greeting "Merry Christmas" to the national conversation. Actually, it never left. "Happy Holidays" is a way to wish seasonal greetings to people of all religions or no religion. It has been a sore spot for about a hundred years on whether the United States is a Christian or secular nation. According to the fact-checking site Snopes, "there is no actual conspiracy to erase Christmas and destroy American civilization in the process ... Belief in a 'War on Christmas' seems to go hand-in-hand with the belief" in Christian nationalism.

49 What is Christian nationalism?

This is the religious and political belief that the United States is fundamentally a Christian nation. It holds that the country is weakened by non-Christians and secularism. Christian nationalists feel threatened by immigration and unbiblical gender identities and sexual orientations. Politically, Christian nationalists have framed the debate as one of patriotism and good versus evil. Pew reported in 2022 that about 60 percent of adults surveyed said they think the founders intended the U.S. to be a Christian nation. Forty-five percent said they think the country should be a Christian nation. A third said the U.S. is a Christian nation now.

50 Are nonreligious people trying to force churches to close?

Most nonreligious people are not. That would go against the spirit of religious freedom. What they would like is to not have to support religion and see it hold advantages such as tax exemptions. Some religious people see this as a threat.

Education

51 What is secular public education?

Secular education emphasizes the separation of church and state within schools. A secular public school establishes a curriculum free from religious dominance. Science is part of the study plan. The U.S. Department of Education established guidelines for secular public schools that emphasize neutrality on religion in schools. It states that students may engage in religious activity and discussion on their own, but schools may not favor or disfavor any set of beliefs.

52 What are secular education's values?

Secular schools are meant to respect all people and religious views. They promote freedom of thought and help develop a moral and humanistic outlook on the world. Michael Nugent, founder of Atheist Ireland, describes secular education as respecting human rights. He said it should neither promote nor discourage religion. Students are left to form their own beliefs outside of school.

53 Is the creation/evolution debate about religion?

Mostly, yes. Pew's research shows much of the debate stems from theological implications and that evolution contradicts the biblical creation story. In addition to religious critics, some individuals see the "survival of the fittest" aspect in the theory of evolution to be socially and politically damaging. This is due to individuals using the theory as justification for actions that hurt others.

54 May public schools teach about religion?

It's all about the context. Discussion and study about religions is important because they intersect with history and society. However, schools and their employees should not speak for or against specific religions and their positions. There is a major distinction between teaching religious values and teaching "about religion," which can be appropriate and permissible. In the 1987 case Edwards v. Aguillard, the U.S. Supreme Court prohibited the teachings of creationism and intelligent design in schools. It was seen as unconstitutionally endorsing religious beliefs over scientific studies.

55 Do schools teach about atheism, too?

In the curricula, atheism should be treated similarly to religions. Promoting or excluding any specific belief is not permitted, and that includes atheism. Learning about religion and nonreligion in public schools should happen in context. These topics may come up naturally in social studies, history, art and literature. This is permissible. Some people are concerned when beliefs are omitted from contexts where they should be addressed.

56 May teachers refuse to teach about religion?

Teachers are required to teach the curriculum, regardless of their personal beliefs. Many cases regarding this issue have been brought to court. They are typically rejected. The Freedom Forum Institute, which focuses on First Amendment rights, said teachers do not have a constitutional right to instill or inhibit religious views in their students.

57 May schoolchildren decline to say the Pledge of Allegiance?

The issue is about requiring children to affirm "one nation under God," and the issue is unsettled. A U.S. appeals court had ruled that Congress' addition of "under God" to the pledge and requiring it to be said in school violate the establishment clause. The case went to the Supreme Court as Elk Grove Unified School District v. Newdow in 2004. The court dismissed the case. It said the father who sued did not have sufficient custody of his daughter to sue.

58 Are voluntary prayer and meditation allowed in public schools?

In 1984, the Supreme Court struck down an Alabama law requiring silent time for "meditation or voluntary prayer." In Wallace v. Jaffree, the court considered whether the state's intention was to endorse or disapprove of religion. The court concluded the law violated religious neutrality.

59 Do nonreligious people feel comfortable discussing faith?

As we've seen, nonreligious people can be quite knowledgeable about religions. Many come from faith traditions and did a lot of thinking before they chose their current identity. But keep your mind and ears open. Trying to use a discussion to convert or criticize is a conversation killer. This often happens to religiously unaffiliated people, so they might be wary.

Milestones

60 What was the original reason for religious freedom?

In the 1700s, religious freedom was a revolutionary change in the relationship between government and faith. Architects of the new government opposed what had been commonplace in European governance. It had denied people representation and led to religious persecution. Religious freedom is enshrined in the First Amendment, which prohibits the government from influencing an individual's religion. In essence, it prevents the government from making laws that interfere with religious free practices and establishments. This protects the decision to not join a religion.

61 When did new presidents start swearing on Bibles?

The tradition of swearing on a Bible began with the first president, George Washington. Other elected officials have since used the Bible and other religious texts. Some say that the very act of swearing on a religious text when assuming a government position is contrary to the oath to uphold the Constitution.

62 When and why was "under God" added to the Pledge of Allegiance?

This was part of a U.S. reaction to communism in the 1950s. In 1952, Congress designated a National Day of Prayer. It declared Americans should turn "to God in prayer and meditation at churches ..." Two years later, "under God" was added to the Pledge of Allegiance. When Francis Bellamy wrote the pledge in 1892, he did not include a reference to God.

63 When did "In God we trust" become the U.S. motto?

"In God we trust" was declared the U.S. motto in 1956 when Eisenhower signed a law passed by Congress. It emphasizes civil religion, connecting the secular and the sacred. Therefore, through the motto, the secular realm can have blessed authority.

64 Have there been other times of rising religiosity?

Yes. One was after the Sept. 11, 2001, terrorist attacks. This led to legislation in many states opposing the imposition of Islamic Sharia Law. This occurred although there has been no serious call to adopt Islamic religious law and it would be unconstitutional to do so.

65 When did the number of nonreligious people begin to increase?

Secularism has old roots and began to increase in the United States during the late 20th century. Surveys show that nonreligious adult Americans increased from 21 million in 2007 to 36.1 million in 2014. The recent shift is attributed to generational replacement since most are young adults.

66 Is secularism growing in the world?

On the contrary, Humanists International calls the status of secularism precarious globally. According to its 2022 Freedom of Thought report, only 4 percent of the world's population live where religious and political authorities are clearly separated. This, the report says, can lead to human rights abuses against the nonreligious.

67 In what other ways is religious participation changing?

Religious participation in the country has changed in sweeping ways. For instance, the percentage of Christians dropped from 77 percent in 2009 to 65 percent in 2019. In addition, religious service attendance has declined by 7 percent over the same period.

68 What was the "new atheism?"

In this early 21st century movement, new atheists confidently and openly showed their positions. The effects of religion on a global scale seem to motivate them. Many new atheists elevate reason above faith. They say that faith is a blind trust that lacks evidence.

69 Is the United States more or less religious than other countries?

The United States is more religious with higher levels of prayer than other wealthy countries, according to a Pew analysis. The disparity may be growing. In 2022, census results for Wales and England reported that Christianity had fallen to less than half the population. The nonreligious had increased by 12 percentage points in 10 years to 37.2 percent.

Legal

70 Does freedom from religion have legal support?

Officially, freedom of religion does support freedom from religion. That was established in the 2005 U.S. Supreme Court ruling in McCreary County v. ACLU. The court determined that the First Amendment protects people who do not practice a religion, as well as those who do.

71 Can people be fired for not belonging to a religion?

Title VII of the Civil Rights Act of 1964 says it is unconstitutional to fire someone for their religious beliefs. This encompasses all religions and those who do not practice a religion.

72 Must people believe in God to hold public office?

A person does not have to believe in God to hold public office. Requiring a government employee to profess their belief in a higher power is "unconstitutional encroachment on the freedom of religion." That was established in the unanimous Supreme Court decision Torasco v. Watkins, 1961. However, laws requiring it are still on the books in some states.

73 Are there state-level protections of the right to not follow a religion?

States technically protect the right of an individual to not follow a religion. However, there are discrepancies among states. According to the 2019 State of the Secular States study from American Atheists, 21 states have laws that include "religious exemptions that undermine equality."

74 Have the courts allowed mandatory prayer in public schools?

Mandatory prayer is not allowed in public schools. This is because public schools are funded by local and state governments as well as the federal government. Under the First Amendment, the government cannot establish or force a religion upon citizens.

75 May prayer be required if it is not associated with a particular religion?

In 1962, the Supreme Court ruled in Engel v. Vitale that mandatory prayer, regardless of association or lack thereof, is still unconstitutional.

76 Is it ever legal to pray in school?

Prayer itself is legal in public schools. Students are allowed to have their own prayer circles, pray before athletic games and so forth. However, the school and its faculty may not sponsor or force students to pray.

77 What led to the elimination of required prayer in public schools?

The Supreme Court's ruling on Abington School District v. Schempp in 1963 established mandatory prayer and Bible reading in schools as unconstitutional. The case was a consolidation of two cases. One was brought against the Baltimore City Public School System by Madalyn Murray O'Hair. She named her son as the plaintiff and argued that mandatory reading of Bible verses and recitation of the Lord's Prayer violated the establishment clause. O'Hair rose to prominence and was reviled during the trial. She founded American Atheists in 1963.

78 What is the International Religious Freedom Act?[3]

This 1998 act is a key component of U.S. foreign policy. It is used to impose economic sanctions on other countries and groups. The act has two parts. The first part condemns violations of religious freedom, and supports people's right to freedom of religion. The second part carries the teeth. It reserves U.S. security and development assistance to governments found not to be engaged "in gross violations

---

3   trincoll.edu/Academics/centers/isssc/Pages/default.aspx

of the right to freedom of religion." Countries of particular concern in 2022 included Burma, the People's Republic of China, Cuba, Eritrea, Iran, the Democratic People's Republic of Korea, Nicaragua, Pakistan, Russia, Saudi Arabia, Tajikistan and Turkmenistan. Entities included Boko Haram, some ISIS groups, the Taliban and Russia's Wagner Group

79 What was the Peace Cross?

In 2014, the American Humanist Society sued the American Legion over a cross-shaped memorial in Maryland. The privately funded cross was built on private land in 1925. It honored service members who died in World War I. However, the property was donated to the Maryland-National Capital Park and Planning Commission, becoming state land. The American Humanist Society argued using public funds to maintain religious imagery violates the establishment clause. The Supreme Court ruled 7-2 in favor of the American Legion in 2019. Justice Ruth Bader Ginsburg delivered the dissenting opinion with Justice Sonya Sotomayor. They believed that displaying the cross on public property was an assumed government endorsement.

Political

80 Is nonreligious voting power growing?

Yes, religiously unaffiliated Americans are becoming a larger part of the electorate. According to a Pew article, the percentage of nonreligious voters has almost doubled in the past decade. They made up 15 percent of registered voters in 2008, 18 percent in 2012 and 28 percent in 2019.

81 Are the nonreligious a voting bloc?

The Secular Democrats of America initiated "Humanists for Biden" in 2020. Hemant Mehta, a columnist who writes as The Friendly Atheist, called it the first organized group of secular Americans to support a presidential candidate. The American Atheist Center posts about issues it supports. One is fighting "Abstinence-only until marriage sex education." It also opposes government support for religious healthcare providers that do not provide some reproductive services. The Freethought Equality Fund has a guide for "Nontheist and Allied Candidates" for office. Candidate endorsements, rallies and visits are not a large part of the group's political presence.

82 Is nonaffiliation being used as a political wedge?

This appears to be developing. The Republican Party has claimed the "Party of God" label. While almost half of nonreligious said they were Democrats, Pew reports that 26 percent of nonreligious voters also said they were Republicans. Additionally, 54 percent of Americans said the Republican Party is friendly toward religion, while only 19 percent said the Democratic Party is.

83 Must people belong to a religion to vote?

No, people are not required to claim a religion to be allowed to vote. However, in Alabama, voters are required to sign a "voter declaration" to vote. On this declaration, voters are required to swear by the phrase, "so help me God." This is the only state in the United States that requires such a signature without a secular alternative. It is not constitutionally enforceable but is still on the books.

84 May nonreligious people run for office?

According to the U.S. Constitution, there can be no religious tests for holding public office. However, according to Article 9 in the Tennessee Constitution, "no person who denies the being of God ... shall hold any office." A 2020 Gallup poll indicated that 60 percent of American voters would vote for a "well-qualified" atheist for president.

Size and projected growth of religious groups from 2015 to 2060

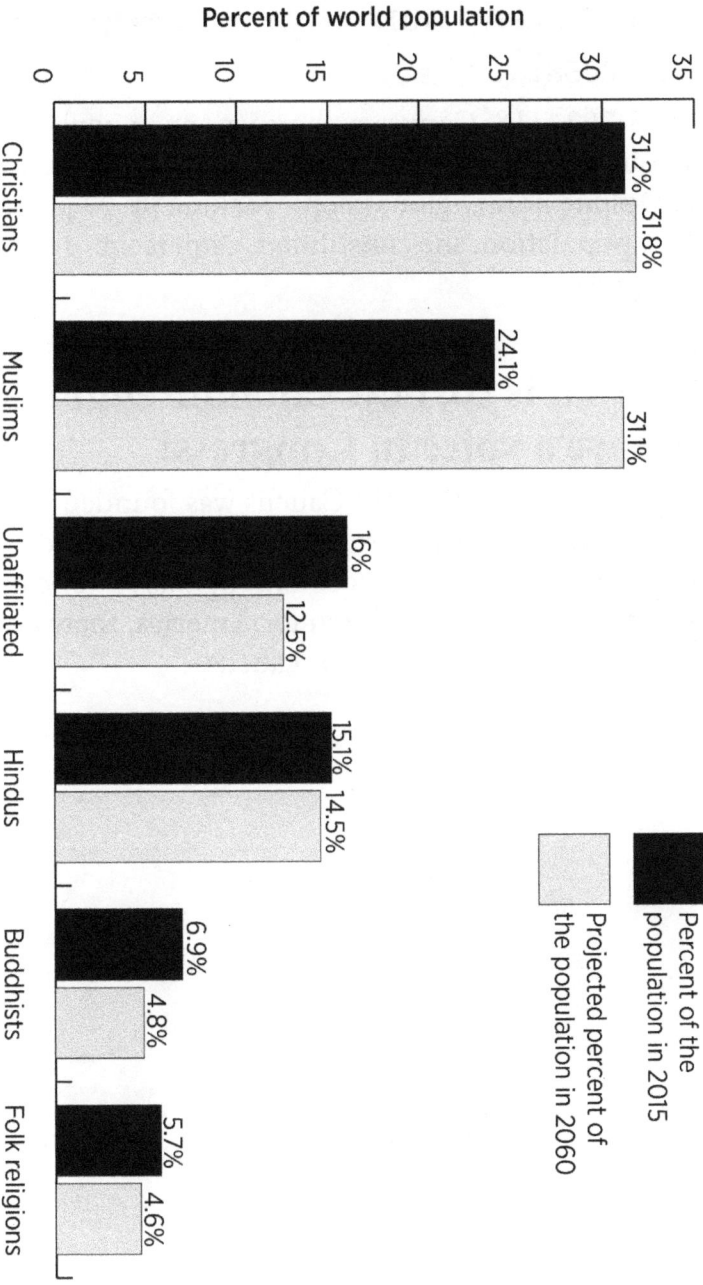

Percent of world population

Legend:
- Percent of the population in 2015
- Projected percent of the population in 2060

Religious group	Percent of the population in 2015	Projected percent of the population in 2060
Christians	31.2%	31.8%
Muslims	24.1%	31.1%
Unaffiliated	16%	12.5%
Hindus	15.1%	14.5%
Buddhists	6.9%	4.8%
Folk religions	5.7%	4.6%

Source: Pew Research Center and World Religion Database

Graphic by Karly Graham

85 How many nonreligious people are in Congress?

In the 2023-2024 U.S. Congress, there was one openly nonreligious person, independent Arizona Sen. Kyrsten Sinema. Despite nonreligious people making up 29 percent of the U.S. population, she constituted 0.2 percent of the 118th Congress.

86 If that is so, how can nonreligious issues have a voice in Congress?

The Congressional Freethought Caucus was founded in 2018. It stands for science, separation of church and state, and equal opportunities for nonreligious Americans. According to the Secular Coalition for America, there are currently 13 representatives in this caucus.

Getting Along

87 How accepting are other Americans of nonreligious people?

Americans are less accepting of their nonreligious neighbors than they are of most religions. According to a survey in which Pew asked people how warmly they felt toward different groups, nonreligious people rated a 50 on Pew's 0-100 "Feeling Thermometer." This was lower than all Christian groups and Jews. The only lower group was Muslims at 48. Warmth toward all groups was up from 2014 to 2017. Almost half of those surveyed said that the growing secularism in the nation is a bad thing. The rest were split between neutral and good.

88 Are children deprived if they do not get to grow up in the church?

The Secular Survey says it is important for children to feel comfortable exploring their spiritual beliefs at home and to practice self-determination. Children in all kinds of families choose paths other than what their parents follow. This question might come from an assumption that children should be exposed to religion. The counter would be to ask religious parents whether they help their children explore secularism.

89 Do people who don't go to places of worship dislike those who do?

Most nonreligious Americans respect the practices of others. Atheists in particular may feel churchgoers are simply wrong in their understanding. What nonreligious Americans dislike is being asked about their church attendance. The Secular Student Alliance encourages young secularists to get active in their community. Its mission is to normalize the identities of those who do not attend houses of worship.

90 Are nonreligious people as patriotic as others?

A Wall Street Journal and NBC News survey reports that the values of patriotism and religion have decreased over the past two decades. God has been added to the national motto "In God We Trust," and the Pledge of Allegiance. When nonreligious people step back, their motives might be misjudged. Religiously unaffiliated Americans do show loyalty to their country. It may be by cherishing its religious freedoms and serving in the military.

91 Are nonreligious people trying to squash faith in America?

That does not seem to be the goal. Their top policy goals do not seek the dissolution of religions. That would seem to compromise their right to not practice religion. The main interest seems to be a desire to be respectfully left alone and to see an end to religious exemptions.

Where the nonreligious experience discrimination

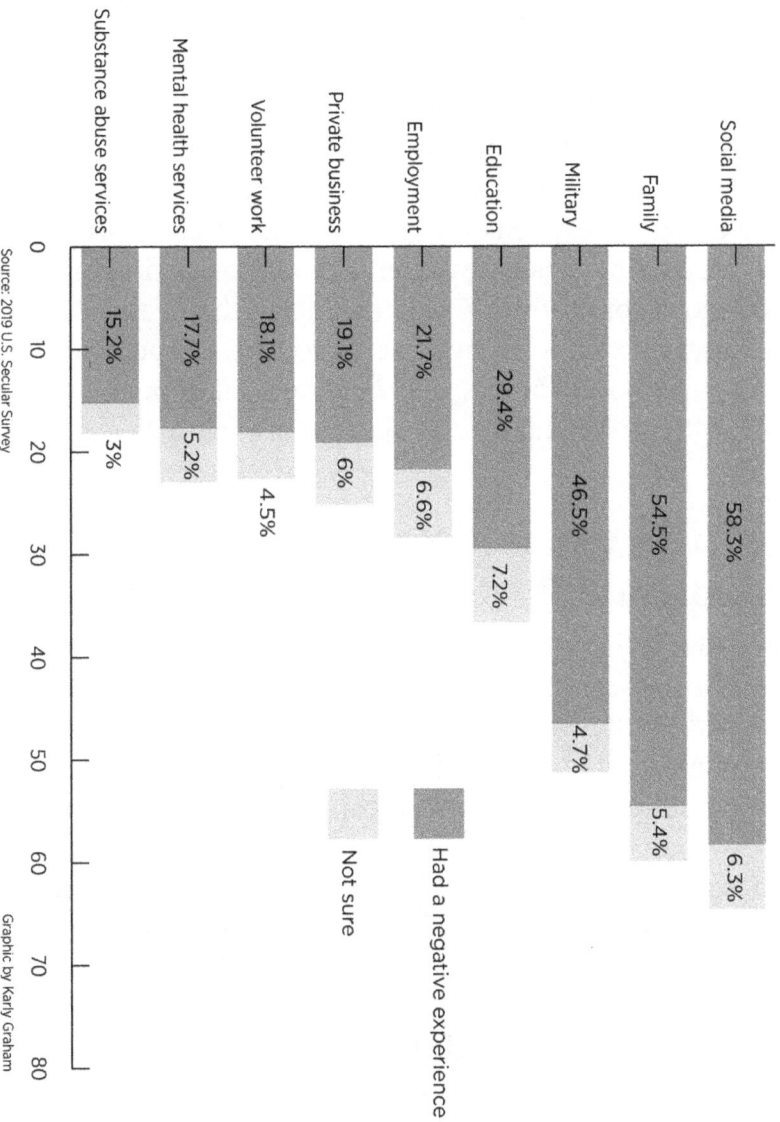

Category	Had a negative experience	Not sure
Social media	58.3%	6.3%
Family	54.5%	5.4%
Military	46.5%	4.7%
Education	29.4%	7.2%
Employment	21.7%	6.6%
Private business	19.1%	6%
Volunteer work	18.1%	4.5%
Mental health services	17.7%	5.2%
Substance abuse services	15.2%	3%

Legend: Had a negative experience / Not sure

X-axis: 0 10 20 30 40 50 60 70 80

Source: 2019 U.S. Secular Survey

Graphic by Karly Graham

92 Do nonreligious people experience discrimination?

A significant number of nonreligious Americans say they experience discrimination. The type, frequency and severity of discrimination varies based upon the religiousness of the surrounding community. Overall, people living in very religious communities were more likely to experience negative events than those living in less religious communities. Participants in the Reality Check survey conducted by American Atheists spoke of getting passed over for jobs and employment opportunities and of getting physical threats because of their beliefs.

93 How else is discrimination demonstrated?

It can show up in laws. According to the American Humanist Association, Texas, Arkansas, Mississippi, Tennessee, South Carolina, Pennsylvania and Maryland have unenforceable laws that prohibit atheists from holding public office. It can show up in families. In the Secular Survey, almost half of Americans say they would be unhappy if a family member married an atheist. Some respondents said members of their extended family will no longer speak to them as a result of their nonbelief. It can show up in society. Nonreligious Hispanic respondents were 77.3 percent more likely than other Hispanic participants to experience assault because of their nonreligious identity.

94 Is harassment of the nonreligious growing?

While Americans are more accepting of nonreligious people than ever, the volume of harassment and crimes against them has also grown. The FBI reported a rise in hate crimes against the nonreligious in 2017. Pew Research reported that the number of countries where nonreligious people were harassed was significantly higher in 2017 than in 2012.

95 Do nonreligious people hide their beliefs?

Almost one-third of nonreligious Americans do not disclose their religious beliefs to one or more members of their immediate family, according to the 2019 Secular Survey. Even more, 44.3 percent, keep their religion a secret from coworkers, and 42.8 percent hide their beliefs at school. This does, of course, indicate that over half of nonreligious Americans are comfortable, or do share their faith with others. Still, others will keep their opinions to themselves while exploring their spirituality with close peers and company.

96 How does this affect them?

The nonreligious may experience loneliness, depression, pressure to fake religiousness, and workplace discrimination. It can happen at home. About 29 percent of respondents under 25 say parents or guardians are somewhat or very unsupportive. Nonbelievers with unsupportive parents had a 71.2 percent greater chance of depression than nonbelievers with supportive parents. Forty-seven and a half percent of Secular Survey respondents reported feeling pressure to pretend to be religious.

97 Is intolerance of nonreligious people an issue in the military?

Among service members who responded to the Reality Check survey, 46.5 percent reported having a negative experience related to their lack of religious beliefs. About a quarter of all military members that responded to the survey said they had dissatisfactory interactions with their military chaplains. In contrast, only 13.5 percent of nonreligious service members had satisfactory relationships with their military chaplains. Some women report that when they were in the service, they were denied contraception for religious reasons. The Secular Survey reported that nearly half of nonreligious servicemembers and veterans had negative experiences while serving.

98 What does unchurched mean?

"Unchurched" and "unmosqued" have been used to refer to people who left religions. But be careful. The labels have acquired negative connotations, such as uneducated, uncultured or impolite. Today, some use the term to refer to Christians who rarely attend church. Unchurched can also mean someone who does not have much experience with church. Remember that many unaffiliated people grew up in an organized religion and that they may know more about religion than other people.

99 Is it OK to invite nonreligious people to services?

Some unaffiliated people say this happens a lot, and it bothers them. It can come across as a negative judgment and a not-so-subtle hint that they should "sign up." Unless a nonreligious person asks to be invited, it is kinder not to initiate an invitation.

100 Can it be offensive to offer to pray for a nonreligious person?

That would deny the beliefs of the person you want to support, which can offend them. To show you care, do or say something that shows you respect them. This can extend to greetings and other sentiments. Rather than "God bless you," or "God willing," use "Peace," "Best wishes," "I support you" or "Safe travels."

For Discussion and Reflection

This guide should be only a first step. We hope you take the next one. That can be an honest conversation with a nonreligious friend, neighbor or co-worker. This can lead to greater understanding and a fuller friendship. But you'll need a few ground rules. One is to listen more than you talk. Another is to be intent on learning. Don't judge. Do not go into the conversation planning to "win." No one is right; no one is wrong. Everyone can win. Third, know that many nonreligious people have had the experience of talking with friends who wanted to "just chat," only to find out their friend actually wanted to convert them or got carried away. That is being a false friend.

If you read this guide, you now know there are many reasons and ways to live without religion. You know, too, that unaffiliated people may or may not believe in God. So, listen to understand, and resist the urge to put people into a box. That habit of labeling beliefs can be bothersome, and it can prevent us from hearing. Let people describe themselves and their ideas in their own ways.

A good discussion about just one or two of these questions can teach you more than the 100 answers in this guide.

- Even though the religiously unaffiliated do not belong to churches, synagogues, mosques or temples, they often form strong community bonds in places like schools, service organizations and even book clubs and gyms. Where can people find or create strong bonds in nonreligious activities?

- It is common to say "I'm praying for you" when a friend is going through a hard time. This can make some religiously unaffiliated people uncomfortable. What are nonreligious ways to express support for nonreligious people? What could you say when you just don't know a person's religious affiliation?

- The United States is officially secular, but references to God are everywhere. They are in the Pledge of Allegiance and "In God We Trust" on our currency. What are other ways government institutions bring religion into daily life? Has it ever made you uncomfortable? Or is it comforting and supportive? Would it be different if the references were to a religion other than your own?

- Many unaffiliated Americans were raised in religious households but left their faith when they got older. How do your beliefs differ from those of your childhood? What shaped these differences?

- While the religiously unaffiliated do not observe religious traditions, some find comfort in rituals. Some rituals can be as simple as taking a morning walk, gathering with friends for dinner once a week or journaling in the evening. What are some nonspiritual practices that bring you peace in your daily life?

- In a 2019 study by the Pew Research Center, nonreligious Americans performed better on a religious knowledge test than their religious peers. Nonreligious Americans also tend to be well-educated. How much do you know about other religions? How does learning about other religious groups shape our beliefs?
- Congress adopted "In God We Trust" as a motto in 1956. Some religiously unaffiliated people find this to be an inappropriate government intrusion. They say it violates the first 10 words of the First Amendment: "Congress shall make no law respecting an establishment of religion …" What do you think? Is mentioning God the same as establishing religion? What is the purpose of having a national motto? What would be a better one? Should there be none?
- Some nonreligious people say stereotypes about them lead to discrimination. What stereotypes might they be talking about? Where do these come from? Have you ever perceived unfair stereotypes about your own beliefs? If yes, how did they make you feel?
- When it comes to talk about a war on Christmas, a 2013 Pew study showed that more than 80 percent of non-Christians celebrated the holiday. The study showed 87 percent of the nonreligious celebrated Christmas. That raises questions about the meaning of Christmas. What ways do people celebrate Christmas? Does it divide us or unite us?
- All of us learn values from nonreligious sources. What other places teach values? Do values need to be taught explicitly or formally?

- Many people stick with religion despite serious misgivings. Why is this? Do questioning and introspection have a place in organized religion?
- When you first learned a friend or relative was nonreligious, what did you think? Did it change the way you felt about them?

Resources

Books

There are a number of books about the religiously unaffiliated. Choose books with care, as most have an agenda and some of them disparage other points of view. There are books that explain the choice to be unaffiliated even-handedly, books that largely criticize people in organized religions, and books, some from Christian publishers, that come from the perspective of proselytizing and conversion.

Claassen, Ryan L. Godless Democrats and Pious Republicans?: Party Activists, Party Capture, and the "God Gap" (Cambridge Studies in Social Theory, Religion and Politics) Paperback. 2015.

Dawkins, Richard. The God Delusion (reprint edition). New York City: Mariner Books. 2008.

Epstein, Greg. Good Without God: What a Billion Nonreligious People Do Believe. New York City: William Morrow Paperbacks reissue. 2010.

Graham, Oppy. Atheism and Agnosticism (Elements in the Philosophy of Religion). Cambridge: Cambridge University Press. 2018.

Hitchens, Christopher. The Portable Atheist: Essential Readings for the Nonbeliever. Boston: De Capo Press. 2007.

Ingman, Neel and Mark Ingman. Not Very Intelligent Design: On the Origin, Creation and Evolution of the Theory of Intelligent Design. Palaceno House. 2018.

Janke, Nick Seneca. Spiritual Atheist: A Quest To Unite Science And Wisdom Into A Radical New Life Philosophy to

Thrive In The Digital Age. Switch on Worldwide Ltd; 2nd ed. 2018.

Keysar, Ariela. Barry A. Kosmin. Religion in a Free Market: Religious and Non-Religious Americans Who, What, Why, Where. Rochester: Paramount Market Publishing, Inc., 2006.

Manning, Christel J. Losing Our Religion: How Unaffiliated Parents Are Raising Their Children. New York City: NYU Press. 2015.

Mehta, Hemant. The Young Atheist's Survival Guide: Helping Secular Students Thrive. Englewood: Patheos Press. 2009.

Prothero, Stephen. God Is Not One: The Eight Rival Religions That Run the World. New York City: HarperOne. 2011.

Smith, Christian and Melinda Lundquist Denton. Soul Searching: The Religious and Spiritual Lives of American Teenagers. Oxford: Oxford University Press reprint. 2009.

ter Kuile, Casper. The Power of Ritual: Turning Everyday Activities into Soulful Practices. New York City: HarperOne. 2020.

White, James Emery. The Rise of the Nones: Understanding and Reaching the Religiously Unaffiliated. Ada: Baker Publishing Group. 2014.

Zuckerman, Phil. Living the Secular Life: New Answers to Old Questions. New York City: Penguin Books. 2014.

Zuckerman, Phil, Luke W. Galen and Frank L. Pasquale. The Nonreligious: Understanding Secular People and Societies. Oxford: Oxford University Press. 2016.

Organizations

American Atheists
https://www.atheists.org/

American Ethical Union
https://aeu.org/

American Humanist Association
https://americanhumanist.org/

Americans United for Separation of Church and State
https://www.au.org/

Atheist Alliance of America
https://www.atheistallianceamerica.org/

Black Nonbelievers
https://blacknonbelievers.com/

Camp Quest
https://www.campquest.org/

Center for Inquiry
https://centerforinquiry.org/

Ex-Muslims of North America
https://exmuslims.org/

Foundation Beyond Belief
https://foundationbeyondbelief.org/

Freedom From Religion Foundation
https://ffrf.org/news/freethought-matters

The Freethought Society
https://www.ftsociety.org/

Hispanic American Freethinkers
https://www.hafree.org/

Institute for the Study of Secularism in Society and Culture
https://digitalrepository.trincoll.edu/isssc/

Military Association of Atheists and Freethinkers
http://militaryatheists.org/

Pitzer College Secular Studies Program
https://www.pitzer.edu/academics/field-groups/
secular-studies/

Recovering from Religion
https://www.recoveringfromreligion.org/

Secular Coalition for America
https://secular.org/

Secular Student Alliance
https://secularstudents.org/

Society for Humanistic Judaism
https://shj.org/

Unitarian Universalists Humanist Association
http://huumanists.org/

Our Story

The 100 Questions and Answers series springs from the idea that good journalism should increase cross-cultural competence and understanding. Most of our guides are created by Michigan State University journalism students.

We use journalistic interviews to surface the simple, everyday questions that people have about each other but might be afraid to ask. We use research and reporting to get the answers and then put them where people can find them, read them and learn about each other.

These cultural competence guides are meant to be conversation starters. We want people to use these guides to get some baseline understanding and to feel comfortable asking more questions. We put a resources section in every guide we make and we arrange community conversations. While the guides can answer questions in private, they are meant to spark discussions.

Making these has taught us that people are not that different from each other. People share more similarities than differences. We all want the same things for ourselves and for our families. We want to be accepted, respected and understood.

Please email your thoughts and suggestions to series editor Joe Grimm at joe.grimm@gmail.com, at the Michigan State University School of Journalism.

Related Books

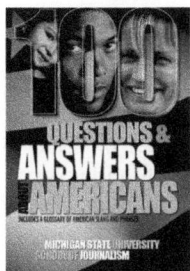

100 Questions and Answers About Americans
Michigan State University School of Journalism, 2013

This guide answers some of the first questions asked by newcomers to the United States. Questions represent dozens of nationalities coming from Africa, Asia, Australia, Europe and North and South America. Good for international students, guests and new immigrants.

ISBN: 978-1-939880-20-8

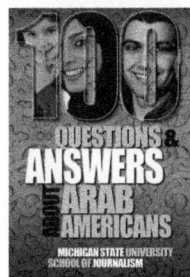

100 Questions and Answers About Arab Americans
Michigan State University School of Journalism, 2014

The terror attacks of Sept. 11, 2001, propelled these Americans into a difficult position where they are victimized twice. The guide addresses stereotypes, bias and misinformation. Key subjects are origins, religion, language and customs. A map shows places of national origin.

ISBN: 978-1-939880-56-7

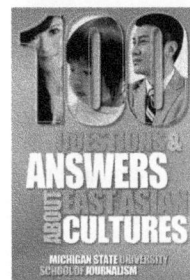

100 Questions and Answers About East Asian Cultures
Michigan State University School of Journalism, 2014

Large university enrollments from Asia prompted this guide as an aid for understanding cultural differences. The focus is on people from China, Japan, Korea and Taiwan and includes Mongolia, Hong Kong and Macau. The guide includes history, language, values, religion, foods and more.

ISBN: 978-939880-50-5

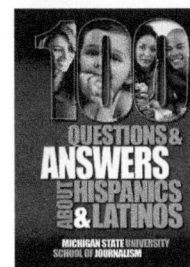

100 Questions and Answers About Hispanics & Latinos
Michigan State University School of Journalism, 2014

This group became the largest ethnic minority in the United States in 2014 and this guide answers many of the basic questions about it. Questions were suggested by Hispanics and Latinos. Includes maps and charts on origin and size of various Hispanic populations.

ISBN: 978-1-939880-44-4

Print and ebooks available on Amazon.com and other retailers.

Related Books

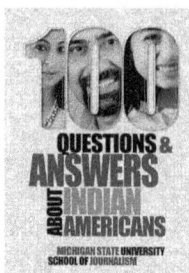

100 Questions and Answers About Indian Americans
Michigan State University School of Journalism, 2013

In answering questions about Indian Americans, this guide also addresses Pakistanis, Bangladeshis and others from South Asia. The guide covers religion, issues of history, colonization and national partitioning, offshoring and immigration, income, education, language and family.

ISBN: 978-1-939880-00-0 m

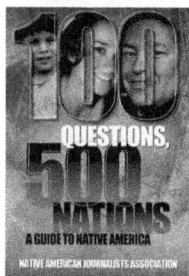

100 Questions, 500 Nations: A Guide to Native America
Michigan State University School of Journalism, 2014

This guide was created in partnership with the Native American Journalists Association. The guide covers tribal sovereignty, treaties and gaming, in addition to answers about population, religion, U.S. policies and politics. The guide includes the list of federally recognized tribes.

ISBN: 978-1-939880-38-3

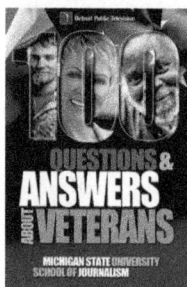

100 Questions and Answers About Veterans
Michigan State University School of Journalism, 2015

This guide treats the more than 20 million U.S. military veterans as a cultural group with distinctive training, experiences and jargon. Graphics depict attitudes, adjustment challenges, rank, income and demographics. Includes six video interviews by Detroit Public Television.

ISBN: 978-1-942011-00-2

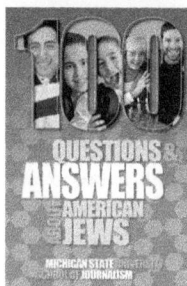

100 Questions and Answers About American Jews
Michigan State University School of Journalism, 2016

We begin by asking and answering what it means to be Jewish in America. The answers to these wide-ranging, base-level questions will ground most people and set them up for meaningful conversations with Jewish acquaintances.

ISBN: 978-1-942011-22-4

news.jrn.msu.edu/culturalcompetence

Related Books

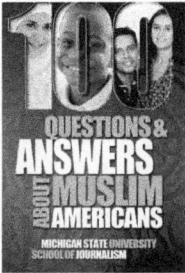

100 Questions and Answers About Muslim Americans
Michigan State University School of Journalism, 2014

This guide was done at a time of rising intolerance in the United States toward Muslims. The guide describes the presence of this religious group around the world and inside the United States. It includes audio on how to pronounce some basic Muslim words.

ISBN: 978-1-939880-79-6

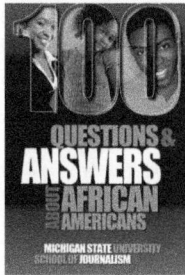

100 Questions and Answers About African Americans
Michigan State University School of Journalism, 2016

Learn about the racial issues that W.E.B. DuBois said in 1900 would be the big challenge for the 20th century. This guide explores Black and African American identity, history, language, contributions and more. Learn more about current issues in American cities and campuses.

ISBN: 978-1-942011-19-4

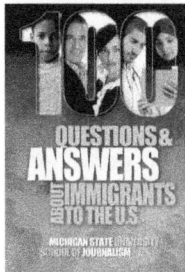

100 Questions and Answers About Immigrants to the U.S.
Michigan State University School of Journalism, 2016

This simple, introductory guide answers 100 of the basic questions people ask about U.S. immigrants and immigration in everyday conversation. It has answers about identity, language, religion, culture, customs, social norms, economics, politics, education, work, families and food.

ISBN: 978-1-934879-63-4

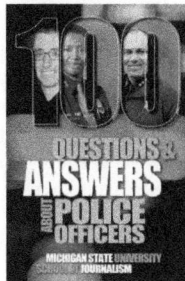

100 Questions and Answers about Police Officers
Michigan State University School of Journalism, 2018

This simple, introductory guide answers 100 of the basic questions people ask about police officers, sheriff's deputies, public safety officers and tribal police. It focuses on policing at the local level, where procedures vary from coast to coast. The guide includes a resource about traffic stops.

ISBN: 978-1-64180-013-6

Print and ebooks available on Amazon.com and other retailers.

Related Books

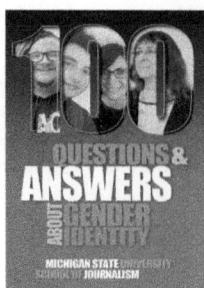

100 Questions and Answers About Gender Identity
Michigan State University School of Journalism, 2017

The guide is written for anyone who wants quick answers to basic, introductory questions about transgender people. It is a starting point people who want to get a fast grounding in the facts.

ISBN: 978-1-641800-02-0

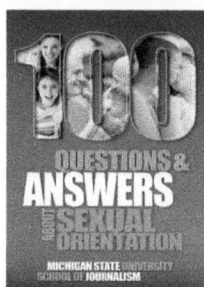

100 Questions and Answers About Sexual Orientation
Michigan State University School of Journalism, 2018

This clear, introductory guide answers 100 of the basic questions people ask about people who are lesbian, gay, bisexual or who have other sexual orientations. The questions come from interviews with people who say these are issues they frequently get asked about or wish people knew more about.

ISBN: 978-1-641800-27-3

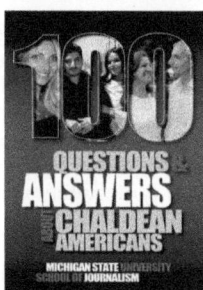

100 Questions and Answers About Chaldean Americans
Michigan State University School of Journalism, 2019

This guide has sections on identity, language, religion, culture, customs, social norms, economics, politics, education, work, families and food. It is written for those who want authoritative answers to basic, questions about this immigrant group from Iraq.

ISBN: 978-1-934879-63-4

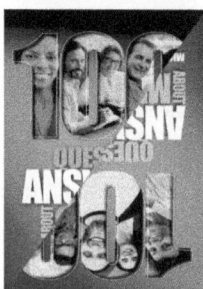

100 Questions and Answers About Gen X Plus
100 Questions and Answers About Millennials
Michigan State University School of Journalism, 2019

This is a double guide in the Bias Busters series. It is written for those who want authoritative answers about these important generations and how we all work together.

ISBN: 978-1-641800-47-1

news.jrn.msu.edu/culturalcompetence

Related Books

True Border: 100 Questions and Answers About the U.S.-Mexico Frontera
Borderzine: Reporting Across Fronteras, 2020

This guide was developed by the University of Texas/ Borderzine for the Bias Busters cultural competence series. The guide is written for people who want authoritative answers about the U.S.-Mexico border region and get up to speed quickly on this important topic.

ISBN: 978-1-641800-60-0

100 Questions and Answers About Latter-day Saints
Michigan State University School of Journalism, 2020

This guide is written for those who want authoritative answers to basic questions about the Latter-day Saints faith. It relies extensively on the Church of Jesus Christ of Latter-day Saints writings and suggests resources for greater depth.

ISBN: 978-1-641800-90-7

100 Questions and Answers About Sikh Americans
Michigan State University School of Journalism, 2022

Sikhism is the fifth largest religion in the world. It is a young religion, having been founded in 1469. It has been in the United States for almost 150 years, but is still relatively unknown. The questions in this guide were created by interviewing Sikhs.

ISBN: 978-1-641801-43-0

100 Questions and Answers About The Black Church
Michigan State University School of Journalism, 2022

Forged in the furnace of U.S. segregation, the Black Church is the pillar of African American communities across the country. This guide answers the call that TIME magazine raised in a headline, "To understand America, you need to understand the Black Church."

ISBN: 978-1-641801-55-3

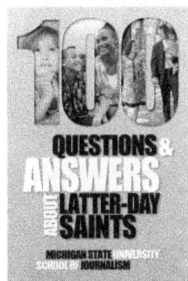

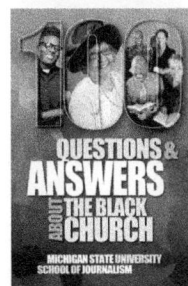

Print and ebooks available on Amazon.com and other retailers.